595

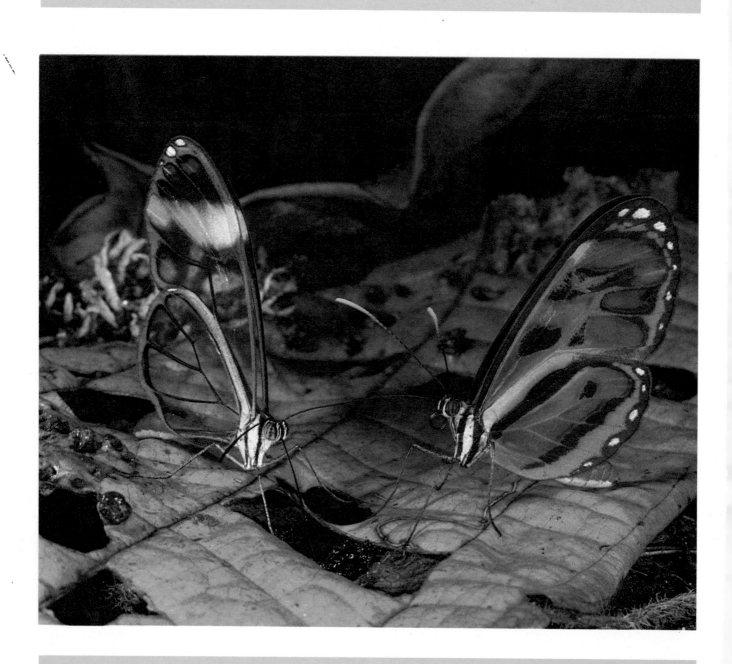

BUTTERFLIES AND MOTHS

Anne Smith

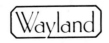

Nature Study

Ants
Bees and Wasps
Butterflies and Moths
Frogs and Toads

Rabbits and Hares
Snakes and Lizards
Spiders
Worms

All photographs from Oxford Scientific Films

Editor: Joanne Jessop

First published in 1990 by
Wayland (Publishers) Limited
61 Western Road, Hove
East Sussex BN3 1JD, England

Originally published in 1986 as
Discovering Butterflies and Moths by
Keith Porter

© Copyright 1990 Wayland (Publishers) Limited

British Library Cataloguing in Publication Data
Smith, Anne
   Butterflies and moths
   1. Butterflies and moths
   I. Title   II. Series
   595.78

   ISBN 1–85210–834–7

Typeset by Kalligraphics Ltd, Horley, Surrey.
Printed in Italy by G. Canale and C.S.p.A., Turin.
Bound by A.G.M., France.

Cover: A British cinnabar moth resting on a ragwort flower. This is one kind of moth that flies by day.

Frontispiece: Clearwing butterflies feeding on the forest floor.

Contents

All words that appear in
bold in the text are
explained in the glossary.

1 Introducing butterflies and moths

A tortoiseshell butterfly.

Butterflies and moths belong to a group of animals called insects. An insect has three main body parts – the head, the **thorax** and the **abdomen**. The head is at the front of the body. The thorax is the middle of the body. The legs and wings grow from the thorax. The abdomen is at the back. This is the largest part of an insect's body.

Insects do not have bones. Each part of the body is covered with chitin (say 'kite-in'). Chitin forms a hard skin that protects the insect's body.

Butterflies and moths have wings that are covered all over with tiny flat scales. Each scale is coloured. These colours help to make the beautiful patterns on the wings of butterflies and moths.

➡ The feelers on this moth's head help it to taste and smell its surroundings.

The bodies of butterflies and moths

Butterflies and moths have two large eyes on their heads. These are called **compound** eyes because they are made up of thousands of tiny **lenses**.
A butterfly or moth has a pair of feelers called **antennae** on its head. Antennae help insects to taste and smell everything around them. Butterflies have long, thin antennae with knobs at the tips. Some moths have long, hair-like antennae. Others have

◄ This oak silk moth has feelers that look like feathers.

feather-like antennae.
Most butterflies and moths eat **nectar** from flowers. They suck up the nectar through a long, thin tongue called a **proboscis**.

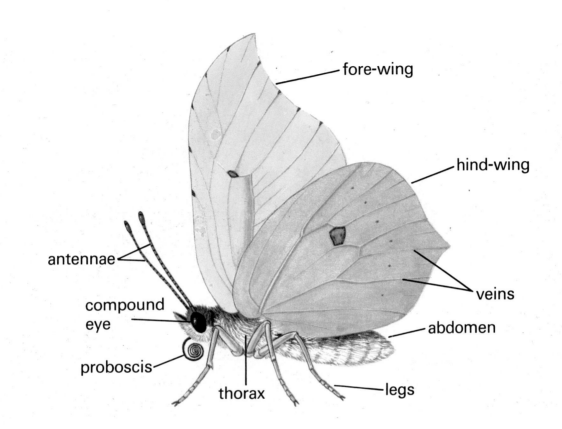

fore-wing

hind-wing

antennae

veins

compound eye

abdomen

proboscis

legs

thorax

This is a brimstone butterfly.

The thorax has strong muscles to move the legs and wings. Like most insects, a butterfly or moth has two pairs of wings and three pairs of legs. The abdomen contains the stomach. Eggs are made in the abdomen.

Different shapes and sizes

There are thousands of different kinds of butterflies and moths in the world. The largest moth is the owlet moth. It measures 30cm across its wings. The smallest moth is only 2mm across. The largest butterfly is the birdwing butterfly.

This is an owlet moth. It is the world's largest moth.

The moon moth has long wing tails.

It measures about 28cm from wing tip to wing tip. The dwarf blue is one of the smallest butterflies. It is about 14mm across.

One way you can tell the difference between a moth and a butterfly is to look at their antennae. But there are other differences. Most butterflies are bright in colour and fly during the day. Moths usually have dull colours and fly at night. A moth rests with its wings out flat. A butterfly rests with its wings together.

Butterflies and moths come in many different colours. Some have clear wings with very little pattern on them. Others have strangely shaped wings with jagged edges or 'tails'.

2
The life cycle of butterflies and moths

A caterpillar hatches from the egg.

From egg to adult

Every butterfly and moth begins life as a tiny egg. A small caterpillar, or **larva**, hatches from the egg. As the caterpillar grows, it bursts out of its old skin and forms a new, larger skin. This happens several times, until the caterpillar stops feeding and turns into a **pupa**.

The pupa is covered with a hard case. Inside the case, the pupa slowly turns into a butterfly or moth. After several weeks or months, the pupa has changed into a fully formed adult butterfly or

moth. It splits open the pupal case and comes out.

At first, the wings of the new butterfly or moth are tiny and crumpled. But they soon fill out. When its wings are dry and hard, the moth or butterfly flies away to feed, find a mate, and lay its eggs.

Most butterflies and moths take a whole year to pass from egg to adult. But some take only a few weeks.

◀ This Gulf fritillary butterfly has just come out of its pupal case.

Life as an egg

The eggs of butterflies and moths are all tiny, but they come in many different shapes. Some look like pearls. Others look

These are cabbage white butterfly eggs.

This is a Gulf fritillary butterfly egg.

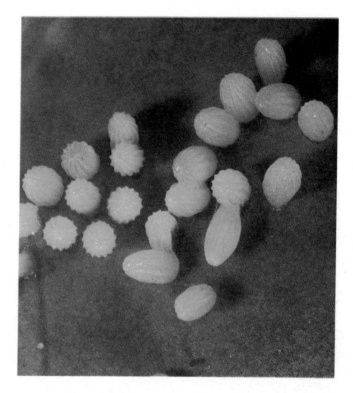

very strange because they have bumps or spikes. Some eggs are coloured and some are clear.

The shell of the egg is made of chitin. It protects the caterpillar that is growing inside the egg. Each egg has a yolk inside. The yolk is used as food for the caterpillar as it grows.

Some types of butterfly and moth eggs hatch after only a few days. Other eggs may take almost nine months to hatch.

Life as a caterpillar

When a caterpillar is ready to hatch, it bites its way out of the shell. Most caterpillars then eat the eggshell before they begin to feed on plants.

Caterpillars have long, soft bodies that are made up of thirteen or fourteen segments. At the front end is a hard,

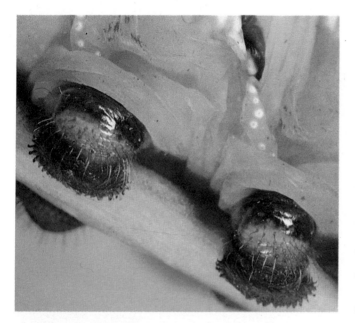

This picture shows a caterpillar's prolegs and the ring of hooks at the end of each proleg.

You can see the jaws of this silk moth caterpillar.

round head with twelve tiny eyes called **simple eyes**.

Caterpillars have eight pairs of legs. The five back pairs are called false legs, or **prolegs**. Each proleg is a soft stump with hooks around the bottom to help the caterpillar cling to leaves or stems. The caterpillar's front three pairs of legs are called true legs. These legs can bend and each leg has a sharp claw at the end.

Caterpillars spend all their time eating. They store food as fat. After about a month, most caterpillars have grown to their full size.

Strange food for caterpillars

Most caterpillars feed on the leaves or stems of plants. Others eat wood, roots or even other insects.

The clothes moth caterpillar feeds on feathers, fur or wool. It is found in old birds' nests, on dead animals, and sometimes in our houses. These caterpillars do a lot of damage because they eat cloth, carpets or curtains. The house moth caterpillar, which is also found in houses, even eats the outsides of tennis balls.

There is a flour moth caterpillar and a meal moth caterpillar that eat our food. There is even a wine moth caterpillar that eats the corks in wine bottles.

◀ This moth caterpillar is eating a sawfly larva.

▶ These wax moth caterpillars are eating the wax in a beehive.

A monarch butterfly pupa.

The change to a pupa

When a caterpillar is fully grown, it stops eating and looks for a good place to change into a pupa. Most butterfly caterpillars look for a firm leaf or a twig. Moth caterpillars dig into plant stems or into the ground.

A butterfly caterpillar starts its change into a pupa by spinning a silk pad on a leaf or twig. It then grips this pad with its last pair of legs. After a while the caterpillar's skin splits open behind its head. The pupa wriggles out of this split in the skin and pushes away the old skin. A butterfly pupa is called a chrysalis.

A moth caterpillar changes into a pupa in a similar way. The big difference is that a moth caterpillar spins a silk case, called a **cocoon**, around itself.

Both the butterfly and the moth pupa are covered with a hard shell. The shell shows the shape of the adult's wings, tongue, legs and abdomen. Inside the pupa, the body of the caterpillar breaks down and then changes into an adult butterfly or moth.

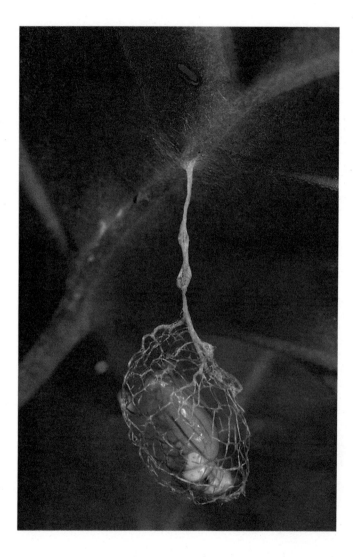

A moth's net cocoon.

3
The daily life of a butterfly or moth

An '89' butterfly.

Resting and feeding

All butterflies and some types of moths spend all day feeding. They sip nectar from flowers or sap from tree trunks. At night they rest among plants and leaves.

Most moths feed and fly only at night. They spend the day resting on tree trunks and among plants. When it gets dark, they leave their hiding places and begin to fly about looking for food.

A moth's body is covered with furry hairs. This helps to keep it warm.

Some moths, like the silk moth, do not feed. They live on the fat that was stored in their bodies when they were caterpillars.

Some butterflies feed on pollen. Others feed on honeydew, which is the thick, sticky liquid made by greenflies.

These moths are feeding on rotting fruit.

These meadow brown butterflies are mating.

Finding a mate

Most adult butterflies and moths live for only a week. During their short lives, they must **mate** and lay eggs to continue the **life cycle**.

Most female butterflies wait with their wings open for a male butterfly to find them. The males are able to find the females of their own kind because of the colour patterns on the females' wings. The female butterfly lets the male know she is ready to mate with a special sign, such as the way she holds her wings. Some types of female butterflies have a special way of flicking their wings to let the males know they are ready to mate.

Moths fly at night and cannot find a mate by sight. They use smell to find a mate. The female moth makes a special scent that the male moth picks up with his antennae. Each kind of female moth has a different smell.

▶ This male zebra butterfly is about to mate with the female butterfly.

Laying eggs

After she has mated, the female moth or butterfly lays her eggs. Most butterflies and moths lay between 100 and 500 eggs. Very few of these eggs will hatch. Most will be eaten by other animals.

Some female butterflies and moths stick their eggs to leaves with a special glue from their bodies. Others carefully

squeeze their eggs into the cracks or holes in plant stems or tree bark. The female chooses a leaf or plant that the caterpillars will be able to feed on when they hatch from the eggs.

◀ This female imperial blue butterfly from Australia is laying her eggs on tree bark.

This female silk moth is laying her eggs.

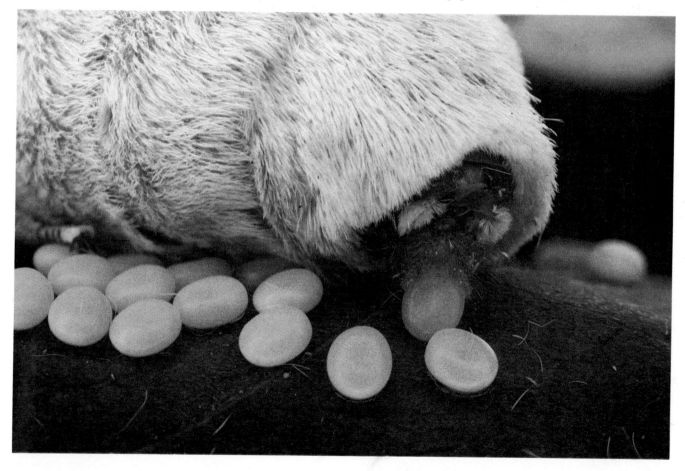

4
Colours have a purpose

A garden tiger moth.

Warning colours

Most butterflies and moths are eaten by birds and other animals. But some moths and butterflies are not eaten because they are poisonous. Most poisonous moths and butterflies are red and black, or yellow and black. These bright colours warn any enemies that these butterflies or moths are nasty to eat.

Poisonous caterpillars also have bright warning colours. Some also have prickly hairs and poisonous spikes as extra protection from their enemies.

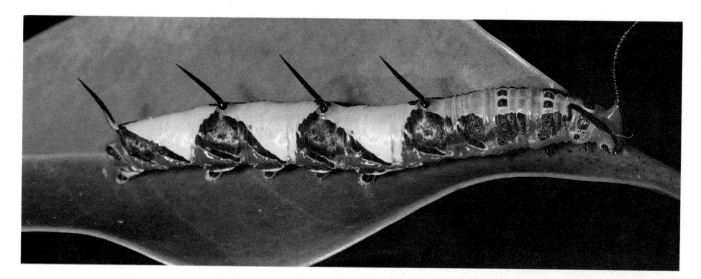

◆ This caterpillar has warning colours and poisonous spikes as extra protection from its enemies.

Tiger moths and burnet moths are very colourful moths. They can fly about safely in the daytime because their bright warning colours show that they are poisonous and warn their enemies to keep away.

Not all brightly coloured butterflies and moths are poisonous. A few types have the same warning colours as the poisonous ones to fool their enemies.

False eyes

Many butterflies and moths have patterns on their bodies that look like eyes. These are called false eyes. False eyes are used to fool an enemy.

When a bird attacks a small animal, it usually goes for the eyes. If a bird attacks a butterfly or a moth with false eyes on its wings, it may end up with only a piece of wing in its mouth. This gives the butterfly or moth a chance to escape.

Some butterflies and moths have large false eyes on each hind wing. These

This owl butterfly has a false eye on each wing.

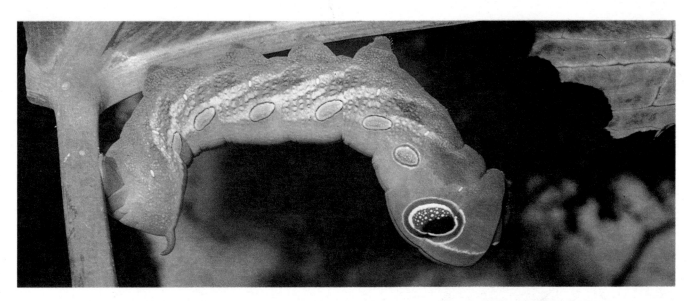

▲ This hawk moth caterpillar scares off its enemies by raising its head to show its large false eyes.

false eyes are usually hidden by the front wings. If an enemy attacks, the moth or butterfly flashes open its hind wings to show two big 'eyes'. This scares away the enemy, who thinks it has attacked a larger animal, perhaps an owl.

A few types of caterpillars have false eyes on the front end of their bodies. These eyes look like those of a snake. This scares off any bird that may attack it.

Camouflage

Many animals have colour patterns on their bodies that help them hide from their enemies. This is called **camouflage**.

Caterpillars are often brown and green. These colours help them to hide among leaves and twigs. Some caterpillars have shapes and colours that make them look like twigs or seed pods. Caterpillars with camouflage keep very still in the daytime. They feed at night, when their movements cannot be seen.

Some butterflies and moths look like dead leaves. The angleshades moth crinkles its wings when it rests to make it look like a dried-up leaf.

◀ This citrus swallowtail caterpillar is not often eaten because it looks like a bird's dropping.

◄ This moth looks like a dead leaf on the forest floor.

Hawk moths use both camouflage and warning colours to escape from their enemies. They have **mottled** front wings to help them hide on tree trunks. Their hind wings are red, blue and orange. When a hawk moth is attacked by an enemy, it flashes its hind wings and frightens its enemy away.

Colours for display

Among the butterflies and moths that find their mates by sight, the males and females are often a different colour. The males usually have bright colours. This helps them to be seen by the females and other males. The females usually have dull colours. This helps the females to hide from their enemies when they are laying their eggs.

Morpho butterflies are a type of butterfly in which the male and female have very different colours. The male morpho has shiny blue wings. This bright colour attracts females. The female has dark brown wings. This colour is a good camouflage in their jungle home.

◀ This bright male chalkhill blue butterfly is about to mate with a female.

◆ The shiny blue colour of this male morpho butterfly attracts females. The female morpho butterfly has dark brown wings.

5
Enemies
all around

A spider catches a peacock butterfly.

Enemies of butterflies and moths

Butterflies and moths have many enemies at each stage of their life cycle. Their eggs are eaten by spiders and insects. Caterpillars and pupae are eaten by birds, lizards, frogs and insects. Adult moths and butterflies are eaten by bats, lizards, birds and other animals.

The eggs of many butterflies and moths are covered with prickly, stinging hairs that keep enemies away. A few types of eggs are poisonous.

◀ This caterpillar is covered with wasp eggs.

Caterpillars often have good camouflage. Others are protected by spines or furry coats. Birds do not like to eat them. Some caterpillars are protected from their enemies because they stay inside stems or rotten wood to feed.

Caterpillars are often attacked by wasps. The wasp sticks a sharp tube inside the caterpillar's body and then lays its eggs. When the wasp eggs hatch, the larvae eat the caterpillar's insides.

Ants and butterflies

Ants are the enemies of many butterflies and moths. They eat eggs, caterpillars, pupae and adults. Some butterflies have a way to stop ants from eating them. The caterpillars

These ants are licking an imperial blue butterfly pupa. The ants like to eat the sweet liquid the pupa makes, but they do not eat the pupa.

This ant is feeding on the sweet liquid made by the imperial blue caterpillar.

and some pupae of these butterflies make a sweet liquid. The ants lick this liquid and do not eat the caterpillars or pupae.

The caterpillars of some butterflies trick the ants into thinking they are ant larvae. The ant takes the caterpillar to its own nest. The caterpillar feeds on the ant larvae. It changes into a pupae, or chrysalis, in the ants' nest. Then it crawls out and flies away as a fully grown adult butterfly.

6
How to study butterflies and moths

A red admiral butterfly.

Gardens are good places to see butterflies and moths. Their caterpillars feed on flowers and vegetables. The adults fly in to feed on flowers.

You may like to grow the flowers that butterflies and moths like best. A very good one is the butterfly bush, or buddleia.

A good way to learn about butterflies and moths is to watch them feed. See which flowers they visit. Watch them push their tongues deep into the flowers. You will have to be quiet and move very slowly.

↥ This little girl and her mother are studying a moth.

You could shine a bright light at night to bring moths into the garden. If you paint a tree trunk or post with a mixture of beer and treacle, moths will come to feed after dark. Moths cannot see red light. So if you cover a torch with red plastic, you can watch them feeding.

Glossary

Abdomen   The rear part of an insect's body. The abdomen is made up of segments.

Antennae   The two feelers on the head of an insect. They are used to touch and smell things.

Camouflage   The colour, pattern or shape that helps an animal to match its background and hide from enemies.

Cocoon   The silk case made by moth caterpillars. The pupa inside the cocoon changes into an adult moth.

Compound eyes   Large eyes that are made up of many tiny lenses. Butterflies, moths and other insects have compound eyes.

Larva   (plural larvae) The grub that hatches from an insect's egg. Moth and butterfly larvae are called caterpillars.

Lenses   The clear parts of an eye that focus light on to the back of the eye to form a picture.

Life cycle   The series of changes, from egg to adult, in the life of an animal.

Mate   To join as male (father) and female (mother). It is how a baby animal is started.

Mottled   Marked with spots or patches of colour.

Nectar   The sugary liquid made by flowers to attract insects.

Proboscis   The long tongue, or mouthpart, of certain insects. It is used for piercing or sucking food.

Prolegs   Short, stumpy legs that are found on caterpillars. They do not bend like true legs.

Pupa   (plural pupae) A stage in the life cycle of an insect when the body of the larva breaks down and then becomes an adult.

Simple eyes   Eyes with only one lens.

Thorax   The second, or middle, part of an insect's body. The legs and wings are on the thorax.

Finding out more

If you would like to find out more about butterflies and moths you could read the following books:

Pat and Helen Clay, *Moths* (A & C Black, 1980).

Oxford Scientific Films, *The Butterfly Cycle* (Andre Deutsch, 1976).

Paul Smart, *The Illustrated Encyclopaedia of the Butterfly World* (Salamander Books, 1976).

V. J. Stanek, *The Illustrated Encyclopaedia of Butterflies and Moths* (Octopus, 1977).

Alan Watson, *Butterflies* (A Kingfisher Guide, 1981).

Paul Whalley, *Butterfly Watching* (Severn House Naturalists Library, 1980).

Ralph Whitlock, *A Closer Look at Butterflies and Moths* (Hamish Hamilton, 1977).

Picture acknowledgements
All photographs from Oxford Scientific Films by the following photographers: G. I. Bernard *frontispiece*, 12, 18, 23, 29, 35; D. Bromhall 38; J. A. L. Cooke 8, 9, 10, 14, 15, 16, 17, 19, 22, 24, 28, 34, 39, 40, 41; Arthur Butler *cover*; S. Dalton 32; M. P. L. Fogden 31, 33; B. Frederick 13; S. Morris 25, 27; K. Porter 36; A. Ramage 20, 21; T. Shepherd 26; G. Thompson 37; P. & W. Ward 30. Artwork by Wendy Meadway.

Index